KU-176-472

My Secret World

Magical Unicorns

Kay Woodward

Illustrated by Strawberrie Donnelly

PUFFIN

PUFFIN BOOKS

Published by the Penguin Group
Penguin Books Ltd, 80 Strand, London WC2R 0RL, England
Penguin Group (USA), Inc., 375 Hudson Street, New York, New York 10014, USA
Penguin Books Australia Ltd, 250 Camberwell Road, Camberwell,
Victoria 3124, Australia
Penguin Books Canada Ltd, 10 Alcorn Avenue, Toronto, Ontario, Canada M4V 3B2
Penguin Books India (P) Ltd, 11 Community Centre, Panchsheel Park,
New Delhi – 110 017, India
Penguin Group (NZ), cnr Airborne and Rosedale Roads, Albany,
Auckland 1310, New Zealand
Penguin Books (South Africa) (Pty) Ltd, 24 Sturdee Avenue,
Rosebank 2196, South Africa

Penguin Books Ltd, Registered Offices: 80 Strand, London WC2R 0RL, England

www.penguin.com

First published 2004
4

Text copyright © Kay Woodward, 2004
Illustrations copyright © Strawberrie Donnelly, 2004
All rights reserved

The moral right of the author and illustrator has been asserted

Set in Weiss
Made and printed in England by Clays Ltd, St Ives plc

Except in the United States of America, this book is sold subject to the condition
that it shall not, by way of trade or otherwise, be lent, re-sold, hired out, or
otherwise circulated without the publisher's prior consent in any form of binding
or cover other than that in which it is published and without a similar condition
including this condition being imposed on the subsequent purchaser

British Library Cataloguing in Publication Data
A CIP catalogue record for this book is available from the British Library

ISBN 0–141–31879–1

Contents

Welcome to the secret world of unicorns . . .

Have you ever wanted to ride away on the smooth back of a magical unicorn? Have you dreamt about stroking its silky mane and whispering secrets into its soft ears? Have you ever imagined flying over the rooftops towards a secret unicorn world that's filled with magic . . .?

Do you think unicorns have special powers? Are they wild or tame creatures? And where do they live?

As you know, unicorns can't be found in zoos. They are only found among the pages of fairy-tale books. They are much, much harder to find in real life. Some people think that they live far, far away in mysterious, misty glades. Others believe that they travel the world, enchanting whoever they meet. A few people say that unicorns don't exist! To find out who is right and who is wrong, take a deep breath and get ready to enter the world of the most spellbinding creature the world has ever seen . . .

Chapter One
The mysterious unicorn

*M*ist swirls and whirls through the shadowy
wood. Drops of moisture glisten on leaves,
branches and blades of grass. Then a shaft of sunlight
pierces the darkness. Slowly, the mist melts away to
reveal a glade among the trees. There stands what
looks like a horse with a sleek, white coat. It raises its
head and the single horn glitters as if it is made of
silver . . .

A unicorn looks very like a horse, but with one
magical difference. It has a magnificent horn on
its forehead.

Throughout history, many claim to have seen

unicorns. Myths and legends have been passed on from generation to generation. These tell about the unicorn's magical powers and dazzling beauty. But not all stories describe the unicorn in the same way. So what does a unicorn really look like?

All the colours of the rainbow

An ancient Chinese myth describes the unicorn as having the body of a deer, horses' hooves and the tail of an ox. The horn was made of flesh, not bone. And it had a multicoloured coat of red, yellow, blue, white and black – the five sacred Chinese colours.

A famous Greek author called Ctesias told of a wild ass that was as big as a horse. It had a white body, purple head and vivid blue eyes. Its horn — which was nearly twice as long as a ruler — was white at the bottom, fading to black, with a bright-red tip. Although many believe that this stunning animal really was a unicorn, it may be that Ctesias actually saw a rhinoceros. But we'll never know . . .

In most stories, the unicorn is said to be pure white. It is sometimes described as having huge silvery-white wings stretching out from its back.

Over the centuries, its description changed and people now think that the unicorn looks much more like a dazzling white horse with white hooves. A single horn spirals out from its smooth forehead.

But, whether these creatures are red, yellow, blue, purple, white or black, all myths tell the same story. Unicorns are beautiful, graceful creatures, surrounded by magic.

Magical unicorn secrets

🍃 The word 'unicorn' comes from Latin words *uni* (meaning 'one') and *cornu* (meaning 'horn').

🍃 A unicorn appears in Harry Potter and the Philosopher's Stone *and also gallops across the cover of* Harry Potter and the Sorcerer's Stone (*the US edition of the same book*).

🍃 Unicorns have beautiful eyes, but it's very difficult to tell what colour they are. Sometimes, they look as if they are chocolatey brown. Sometimes, they look the deepest blue.

Chapter Two
Unicorn secrets

*W*ARNING: *Do not read this chapter in public. Go to a secret, safe place where you won't be disturbed by brothers, sisters, aunties, second cousins or anyone else desperate to learn the unicorn's secrets. Your bedroom would be ideal. Under a duvet in your bedroom would be even better. Now . . . are you alone? Then read on . . .*

Unicorns are very private creatures that go to great lengths to keep their world secret and safe. There have been no official sightings of them for centuries. But, during those centuries,

plenty of people have seen the mythical, magical, mysterious creatures. They just haven't told anyone else that they saw them.

Remember, if you are ever lucky enough to see a unicorn, keep it to yourself. The world is full of people who will never meet the magical being – and will laugh at anyone who has.

Unicorn babies

If you think it's hard to spot a unicorn, it's even harder to spot a baby one. Unicorn foals are kept out of sight until they are old enough and clever enough to look after themselves. By day they frolic in the deepest parts of the world's darkest woods,

while their mothers search for food. By night
they slumber, hidden beneath blankets of moss
and fern, safe from creatures that hunt by
moonlight.

Baby unicorns are not taught to be magical —
they just are. Within a few minutes of being
born, they can run, skip and leap high into the
air. Within an hour, they can talk to the mother
unicorn by thought alone. And, by the time
they are one week old, they can summon a
woodland mist and make tiny berries plump and
ripe with a single bewitching glance.

The language of unicorns

Unicorns are extraordinarily quiet animals.
They can neigh, harrumph, snicker and blow,
just like horses, but mostly they prefer to
remain silent. A unicorn will only utter a sound
if it is in terrible danger from hunters or lions.
Signals, thoughts, feelings or simply information
about the nearest source of food are beamed out

and picked up by all unicorns within a distance of fifty kilometres. Because enemies find it impossible to read the silent signals, the unicorns' secret world remains safe.

🌿 Faster than fairies

Unicorns are among the swiftest beings alive. They are faster than the fastest racehorses and swifter than the swiftest swallow. This speed is all thanks to the unicorns' enchanted hooves. They contain enough magic to whoosh a unicorn to the moon and back – in the blink of an eye.

Some people believe that unicorns have huge, feathery wings – you might see pictures of these in storybooks. Others think that unicorns have no need for wings. They have more than enough magic inside for them to gallop or zoom around the world as fast as a fairy.

Magical unicorn secrets

Unicorns are really ticklish! They have a very sensitive spot just behind their ears.

🍃 Unicorns are so incredibly magical that they do not have red blood like humans. Instead, they have pure liquid silver running through their veins.

🍃 Baby unicorns are born without a horn. The mother and foal stay together until the horn is fully grown, which can take many years.

Chapter Three
The unicorn's horn

The powerful king gasped in delight as the merchant unpacked his wares. He couldn't believe his eyes. His courtiers had searched long and hard, high and low for this. Could it really be a unicorn's horn – at last? He turned the precious object in his hands. 'I must have it, whatever the price . . .' he breathed.

The unicorn is known for its shining, white coat, its cascading mane and flowing tail. But it is the long, silvery horn that really makes it special. Without it, the unicorn might be mistaken for a horse – still beautiful, but not magical.

The power of the horn

There's no other creature on Earth that has a horn like a unicorn. Stretching proudly from its forehead, the horn is decorated with perfect spiral grooves, from top to bottom. In darkness, it glows. In daylight, it dazzles.

But that's not all. A unicorn's horn is not just an orna- ment. It is filled with magic . . . Just by dipping its horn into poisoned water, a unicorn can make it pure and clean once more. A touch of the horn can cure the sick and heal the injured.

It is said that people used to take advantage of the unicorn's amazing healing powers. They

hunted the precious animals and used their horns to cure many illnesses including fever, plague, stomach ache, epilepsy and rabies.

🌸 The secret of the horn . . .

According to legend, there lies a sparkling surprise at the base of a unicorn's horn — a rich-red ruby. Like the horn, this beautiful jewel has many magical powers. It can make sadness disappear and wickedness vanish in a twinkling. It can also banish poison.

The unicorn's jewel is known by many names — as a mystic ruby, a horn stone and a carbuncle. And, mysteriously, only a few special unicorns have such a jewel. These are the oldest and wisest unicorns of all . . .

Real or fake?

Hundreds of years ago, unicorn horns were worth more than their weight in gold. Everyone wanted one, but only the richest could afford them. And merchants travelled the world selling unicorn horns to those who were desperate enough to buy them. After all, a unicorn horn was said to guarantee a long and healthy life.

But there was a problem. Most – if not all – of the unicorn horns were fakes. They were made of bull horn, goat horn or even dog bones. Many of the most unicorn-like 'unicorn horns' came from narwhals – small, toothed

whales that live near the North Pole. One of the narwhal's front teeth develops into a very long tusk, which eager buyers often mistook for a unicorn's horn.

Top-class unicorn experts soon said that they'd solved the problem. They had tests that would show whether a horn came from a unicorn or not . . .

Unicorn Horn Test A

1. Using the unicorn horn, draw a circle on the floor. (This works best on a sandy beach.)
2. Wait for a spider to come along.
3. If the unicorn horn is real, the spider will not be able to cross the circle.
4. If the unicorn horn is fake, the spider will be able to run, jump or jig in the circle and come to no harm.

Unicorn Horn Test B

1. Find a large bowl and fill it with cold water.

2. Place the horn into the water and watch carefully.

3. If the water bubbles, but stays cold, the unicorn horn is real.

4. If the water bubbles and gets warmer, the unicorn horn is fake.

5. If nothing happens at all, the unicorn horn is fake.

Magical unicorn secrets

Two of the most famous people to hand over large piles of gold for a unicorn horn were Pope Paul III and James I of England (James VI of Scotland). With the gold they paid for their treasures, each man could have bought an enormous castle.

If a unicorn's horn is placed near poisoned food, the horn becomes wet.

 Some people believe that a rhino's horn can be used to cure fevers, just like the unicorn's horn. Animal welfare organizations are trying to stop rhinos from being killed for their valuable horns.

Chapter Four
Legends from the East

*W*ith a sigh of relief, the girl sank to the ground beneath the cherry tree. She looked first to the Huozhou Mountains, then up through branches laden with pink blossom. This was perfect. Carefully, she unpacked her most precious book. At once, it fell open at the page she had marvelled over so many times before. She ran her fingers over the delicate Chinese calligraphy, spread the book on her lap and began to read . . .

The pages of storybooks around the world are sprinkled with unicorns. The mystical creatures swoop through fairy tales on silvery wings.

They stand proudly to meet their foes in stories of valour. And they spread magic and goodness wherever they go.

The very first unicorn tales date back hundreds and hundreds of years. And they tell the stories of people who were lucky enough to meet real, true-life unicorns.

The gift of writing

The Chinese emperor Fu Hsi lived almost 5,000 years ago. A good ruler, he was well known for his inventions of musical instruments.

One fine day, Fu Hsi was resting near the banks of Huang He, one of China's longest rivers. Suddenly, his skin began to prickle and he knew that he was being watched. Fu Hsi looked up and saw a small, dainty animal, about the size of a foal standing in the muddy water. But he had never seen a foal with such a coat of shimmering colour, nor a horn that looked as if it were made of pure silver. Then the emperor

noticed with awe that the water around the animal's feet was no longer muddy, but was clear and sparkling.

Fu Hsi was astonished. What was this strange creature? He rose to his feet, but in a flash the animal swiftly moved away. As it went, the emperor saw curious symbols marked on its glorious coat. He scratched his head, thought

for a moment and then scratched the symbols into the soil. According to the legend, these became the first written characters of the Chinese language.

Telling the future

Unicorns do not just dazzle and amaze all who see them; their sudden appearances also show that an important event is about to take place. Confucius was one of China's greatest teachers and thinkers. Before his birth, a unicorn visited his mother. The creature gently laid a piece of jade into her hand. A message engraved on to the precious green stone said that the young woman's son would be a great man. The unicorn's message came true.

Years later, Confucius himself saw a unicorn. But this time, the charmed creature foretold his death . . . How spooky is that?

Magical unicorn secrets

🌿 Not a single unicorn has been seen in China for many years. Many believe that the peace-loving unicorn is hiding deep in the darkest forests, waiting until the world is rid of unhappiness and war. Then it will reappear.

🌿 The hooves of a unicorn make no sound as they touch the ground. Some say this is because they tread very carefully to avoid harming anything.

🌿 In China, the unicorn is often known as a ki-lin.

Chapter Five
Taming the unicorn

*T*he gleaming unicorn galloped through the wild
woods. He rushed like the wind through thickets
and round great oaks, leaping over boughs that lay
strewn in his path. Nothing would halt him. He was
untameable. Unstoppable. Then the amazing
happened: he stopped. There before him was a young
girl, wearing a dress as white as snow. Calmly, she
sat down beneath a tree – and beckoned. Timidly,
the unicorn went to her and laid his smooth head
on her lap.

Unicorns run faster than any horse and are
fiercer than any tiger. There is only one thing in

the whole world that can tame them — a girl
with a pure soul. They alone have the power to
quieten and soothe the wild creature. Perhaps
it's because both are honest, true and very,
very good. Are you good enough to tame a
unicorn . . .?

How to tame a unicorn

Although unicorns have not been seen for
many, many years, they are out there just waiting to be coaxed into view. Here are the steps
you must follow to spend a few magical
moments with a unicorn . . .

*(Sorry, the following only applies to girls. Boys and
unicorns don't mix.)*

1. Wear a spotless white dress. This should be
   so clean that it smells of washing powder and
   so white that it dazzles in daylight.
2. Be prepared — make a set of golden reins to
   hold the unicorn. Yellow or gold wool will
   do.

3. Find a healthy young tree covered with bright new leaves. Is there one in your garden? If not, a bushy plant will do. (Don't go rushing off to the middle of the woods – it is dangerous and you don't want to get your white dress dirty.)

4. Sit beside the tree or plant and clasp your hands together. Now would be a good time to recite a unicorn poem that you've written. Or try shutting your eyes and wishing really, really hard.

5. If a unicorn appears, wait until it lays its head

in your lap, then gently loop the reins round its slender white neck. The unicorn will now allow you to stroke its silky mane.

6. Remember not to hold on to the unicorn for too long. This is a creature that loves to be free.

Magical unicorn secrets

Even the flimsiest golden reins are strong enough to hold a unicorn. A glittering loop is all it takes to make the creature calm and relaxed. Stroking the unicorn's soft nose helps too.

🦋 You might have made a wish after blowing out the candles on your birthday cake. You might have wished upon a star. But have you ever wished on a unicorn? Try it next time you really want something to happen — see if your wish comes true . . .

🦋 If you look up into the sky on a clear winter's night, you will see a unicorn shining there. To find the starry unicorn, look to the east of Orion — one of the brightest constellations in the night sky. This very special constellation Unicornu (now called Monoceros) was named by German astronomer Jakob Bartsch in 1624.

Chapter Six
I spy a unicorn . . .

The Roman general leant forward in his saddle and peered through the trees. He was in the middle of a very important conquest. Thousands of men awaited his command. But here, in Hercynian Forest, Julius Caesar had seen something to make him tingle with excitement – something to make him forget all about blood and war. A handsome creature stood half hidden by leaves – a creature with a long, elegant horn.

You don't have to be an emperor or general to spot a unicorn, but it helps. Over the centuries, great leaders and monarchs have spied the

mythical creature and then told the world about it. Here are just a few of the most famous unicorn-spotters . . .

The terrifying warrior

Genghis Khan, the great Mongolian leader, was fierce, fearless and feared by all who knew him. He and his armies fought their way across Asia, conquering countless countries and killing thousands of people. Nothing stood in Genghis Khan's way – until he tried to invade India. He and his soldiers were trekking through a steep

mountain pass when they were met by a strange vision. A beautiful unicorn galloped swiftly towards the fierce warrior, halting before him. The unicorn bent its knee once, twice, three times as a sign of respect. And the violent, ferocious Genghis Khan was so touched that he decided not to invade India after all — because of a single unicorn.

The great king

Alexander the Great is famous for being a really great king who lived a very short life. But legend says that he achieved a lesser-known feat — taming a unicorn.

When a wild animal with a single horn was captured and given to Alexander the Great's father, the court didn't know what to do with the beast. Some records say that it was a horse, but others believe it was a unicorn. The creature snapped razor-sharp teeth at anyone that came near. And everyone who attempted to climb on

to the unicorn's back was thrown skywards.

Everyone, that is, except the fourteen-year-old Alexander. He tamed the unicorn, named him Bucephalus and rode him into battle.

The Greek philosopher

Aristotle, the ancient Greek thinker and scientist, knew that unicorns were real. After studying evidence from explorers and travellers, he decided that unicorns had solid hooves like horses, despite the fact that he'd never ever seen a real one. But Aristotle was unsure about the unicorn's horn – he did not believe that it was really magic.

Magical unicorn secrets

🌿 St Thomas and St Gregory both wrote about unicorns. They — and other religious people — thought that the unicorn was a holy symbol.

🌿 Unicorns live for a very, very long time — much longer than humans. No one is exactly sure how old the oldest unicorn is, but it may be hundreds of years . . . or even older.

🌿 Alexander the Great's unicorn may actually have been an oryx. This is a large antelope with two horns, but when it stands sideways, it looks as if it only has a single horn.

Chapter Seven
The lion and the unicorn

The unicorn raised its head and looked from beneath snow-white eyelashes. Its enemy was approaching. Not men armed with swords and arrows. Not a herd of stampeding bulls. It was something dangerous enough to threaten the unicorn's fragile world. A lion padded softly into view. Their eyes met. The battle was about to begin.

According to tradition, the lion is the unicorn's biggest enemy. But why should two such splendid animals dislike each other? Because the lion is jealous of the unicorn's magic? Because the unicorn longs to be king of the jungle? No. It's

all to do with the changing of the seasons . . .

🌿 *The battle of the seasons*

Long, long ago, in the ancient kingdom of
Babylon, the people decided that different
animals represented different seasons. The
unicorn represented spring — it was pure and
magical, gently waking up the world after the

cold, dark winter. The lion stood for summer —
bright, golden and full of life.

Each year, the Babylonians believed that there
was a great battle between the unicorn and the
lion. The unicorn loved spring and didn't want
it to end. But each year, the lion fought on
behalf of summer. Even today, the lion wins the
fight every year and summer follows spring.

Bitter enemies
Legend says that the
lion had a clever, but
mean, way of catch-
ing a unicorn. It
would wait patient-
ly in front of a leafy
tree in a sunny glade.
When a unicorn came
near, the lion made fun
of the beautiful animal,

laughed at it and pulled faces at it. The unicorn became so cross that it charged furiously towards the lion – and the lion stepped aside at the last moment. The poor unicorn was left with its horn buried in the tree, totally at the mercy of the lion. And then the lion pounced.

The royal unicorn

In the fourteenth century, the unicorn was given a special honour by a Scottish king. Robert III decided that this lovely animal was the perfect symbol for his country. It was pure and strong and true – just like Scotland. So, the unicorn leapt on to the official coat of arms of the country. Meanwhile, a fierce lion decorated the English coat of arms.

Two hundred years later, the lion and the unicorn came together. When Elizabeth I died, James VI of Scotland became James I of both England and Scotland. James thought that this was the perfect time to link the countries and

their symbols. So he designed a brand new coat of arms with both an English lion and a Scottish unicorn. The lion and the unicorn were united at last – but that didn't mean that they were friends . . .

This well-known nursery rhyme talks about the many battles between England and Scotland:

The lion and the unicorn
Were fighting for the crown.
The lion beat the unicorn
All about the town.

Some gave them white bread,
And some gave them brown,
Some gave them plum cake,
And sent them out of town.

Magical unicorn secrets

A statue of a unicorn stands in St Stephen's Chapel, Westminster Palace in London. The unicorn is held back by a carved chain. Even though it is made of stone, it might still be dangerous.

Did you know that you may be able to spot a unicorn when you're eating your breakfast? The lion-and-unicorn coat of arms appears on all sorts of jars and packets, from jam to breakfast cereal.

Unicorn foals stay with their mothers for about fifty years! By then they are old enough to cope on their own — and it's time for the mother unicorn to bring another baby unicorn into the world.

Chapter Eight
The last unicorn?

Splish! Splash! Splish-splash-splosh! It was as if the rain would never stop. Puddles grew bigger and bigger, until they stretched across whole fields. Rivers burst their banks, sending water gushing through towns and villages. And still the rain fell. Soon, only the highest ground was above water. Desperately, people and animals clambered to safety. Would everyone be saved? Would anyone survive?

Some people believe that unicorns are in hiding, that they will one day reappear to sprinkle their magic throughout the world. But there are others who believe that the very last unicorn

vanished centuries ago. Is this because of global warming? Did they freeze during an ice age? Or did the last unicorns simply miss the boat?

Noah's ark

The Bible tells how the Earth was once a really dreadful place. It was filled with nastiness and spite and crime and violence. God got so fed up with everyone behaving badly that he decided to punish them – and give the world a spring clean at the same time by flooding it with water. But not everyone was bad. God decided to spare Noah – after all, there would have to be some-one left after the waters went down. He told Noah to build a type of ship called an ark. This should be big enough for his family and for two of every type of animal in the world.

When the rain started to fall, Noah and his family welcomed the animals – which came two by two – into the ark. Two lions, two tigers and two elephants climbed on board. There were

two monkeys, two bears, two chickens and two dogs. But there was no sign of any unicorns. The ark got fuller and fuller. Soon, there was hardly room to move. Then the waters began to rise and it was time for Noah and his ark to sail away. The unicorns were too late.

So what happened to the unicorns? Were they too busy playing to listen to Noah? Did they all die in the flood? Or did they find a safe place, out of reach of the water . . .?

Magical unicorn secrets

🌿 Unicorns can gallop, leap and fly through the air, but they cannot swim.

🌿 Unicorns do most of their travelling by moonlight. Most people are asleep, so there is less chance of them being spotted.

🌿 Unicorns love berries — raspberries, blueberries, logan-berries, strawberries, bilberries . . . any sort of berries!

Chapter Nine
Deep in the forest . . .

*T*he eager explorer heaved the bulging rucksack on to her back once more. She was getting closer — she could feel it. The further she trekked from civilization, the closer she travelled towards the secrets of the forest. She might see animals that no one had ever seen before. Or she might collect evidence of a species that everyone thought was extinct. She clutched the camera in her hand and moved forward.

Even though the world has been explored from pole to pole and east to west, new types of animal are still being found. And if these creatures can remain hidden for years, then perhaps

the mysterious
unicorn is in
hiding too. It
might be lurk-
ing in the
middle of a
forest or
sheltering in a
remote mountain
valley, just waiting to
be discovered . . .

Brand new deer

In 1992, in the Vu Quang forest reserve in
northern Vietnam, a brand new animal was
discovered. It wasn't a tiny toad or a teeny turtle
or a microscopic millipede. It was a deer! And
this deer had very special horns – long, straight
and very like the horn belonging to the magical

unicorn. Animal experts were astonished. How could something as big as a deer stay hidden for so long?

But this wasn't all. When explorers looked deeper into Vietnam's forests, they found another totally new type of deer. This one was as big as a large, shaggy dog — and had two short, thick horns.

Both of these deer are very rare. Plans have now been made to make sure that the new deer don't disappear like the unicorn.

Tongue-twisters

These brand new animals have been given brand new names but, unfortunately, they aren't as easy to say as 'unicorn'. Before attempting to pronounce them, it is recommended that you perform the following exercises:

1. Open your mouth into a really wide smile.
2. Close it.

3. Pucker your lips.

4. Move them quickly from side to side.

5. Wiggle your tongue round your mouth, then stick it out.

6. Say 'aaaaaaaah'.

7. Repeat if necessary.

Ready, steady . . .

Pseudoryx nghetinhensis (soo-dor-ix n-get-in-hen-sis)
Megamuntiacus vuquangensis (mega-mun-tee-ak-us voo-kwan-jen-sis)

Wouldn't you love
a name like that?
Well, maybe not . . .

The unicorn dance

At the beginning of the new lunar year in Vietnam, special unicorn dances are performed in the south of the country. Here, the unicorn is

a symbol of peace, happiness and prosperity. A
magnificent model of a unicorn is carried
through each town by jumping, twirling dancers
– followed by a bright, colourful procession.

The unicorn is presented with many gifts –
people are eager to donate money to make sure
that the year ahead will be a good one. But, just
to make things more exciting, the unicorn's gifts
are hung from the top floors of homes and

shops. The dancers have to climb on to each other's shoulders to reach each donation!

Magical unicorn secrets

🍃 Marco Polo, a famous explorer from Venice, was convinced that he'd seen unicorns on his travels. He described a 'unicorn' as being nearly as big as an elephant, with hair like a buffalo and a thick black horn in the middle of its forehead. Unfortunately, this may actually have been a Sumatran rhino.

🍃 When explorers combed through other Vietnamese forests, they also found a new type of pheasant, which now lives in Saigon Zoo.

🍃 A shadhahvar is a bad-tempered unicorn that is said to come from Iran. It has a hollow horn, a little like a flute, which plays a haunting melody when the wind blows through it. The shadhahvar lures its prey with this tuneful horn. However, this animal is as difficult to find as the unicorn — and no one is now sure if it really exists or not.

Chapter Ten
A magical unicorn world

If you love unicorns, why not make these special unicorn treasures for your room? Then, whenever you go there, you'll be reminded of unicorns and all the magic they bring . . .

A magical unicorn mobile

Try adding a touch of sparkle to your room with this dazzling unicorn mobile. Here are some of the things you'll need:

* Two wire coat hangers
* Card
* Some small pieces of tinsel

* Glitter
* A glass prism with a hole at the end
* A small hook that can be screwed into a wall or ceiling
* Silver thread
* Scissors, glue and sticky tape

1. First, make a stencil following the outline on the next page. You could trace the image on to tracing paper and flip the paper over. Then, pressing firmly with a pencil, rub this outline on to a piece of card. Or, if you're feeling more artistic, copy the picture straight on to a piece of card. Cut out the image to make a unicorn-shaped hole. Are you feeling magical yet . . .?

2. Next make the basic mobile shape by crossing the two hangers, while keeping the hooks together. Wind sticky tape round the hooks, then fasten the bottoms of the hangers together too.

3. Now it's time to let your imagination run wild! Decorate your mobile using all the shiny and sparkly things you've gathered together. Why not cut out unicorn shapes, cover them with glitter, then hang these from the mobile with silvery thread? Wind tinsel round the bare wires to hide them . . .

4. When your mobile is totally glittery, decide where to hang it. The space above your window, behind your curtains, is a good spot. And don't forget to check with your mum and dad before making a hole in anything.

5. For a perfect finishing touch, hang a prism from the bottom of the mobile. Then, whenever sun shines into your room, the walls, ceiling, everything will shimmer and dance with all the colours of the rainbow!

🌸 A multicoloured unicorn pen

If you're going to write magical unicorn stories, you'll need a unicorn pen in the shape of a horn. Here's what you'll need:

* ★ Card
* ★ Plates of different sizes
* ★ A pencil
* ★ Scissors
* ★ Felt-tip pens or paints
* ★ Sticky tape
* ★ Plasticine or Blu-Tack
* ★ A cheap pen

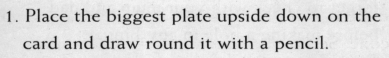

1. Place the biggest plate upside down on the card and draw round it with a pencil.
2. Draw smaller and smaller circles inside the large circle, using all of the other plates.
3. Using felt-tip pens or paints, carefully colour in each of the circles. You could choose the colours of the rainbow – red, orange, yellow,

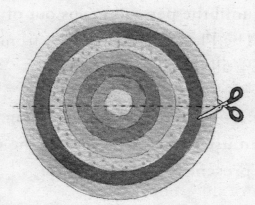

green, blue, indigo and violet – or just a
mixture of your favourite colours.

4. Cut out the largest circle, and
   then cut this circle in half.

5. Take one half and coil it round
   until you have a shape like
   an ice-cream cone. Make sure
   there is a small hole at the bottom of the
   cone. Secure the cone with sticky tape.

6. Now take a small ball of Plasticine or
   Blu-Tack and clump it round the top
   of your pen, near the nib.

7. Nearly there! All you have to do
   now is stick your pen down the

cone until the pen nib peeps out of the end. The Plasticine will stop it from coming all the way through.

Top tip: You could make a matching unicorn-horn pen using the other half of the circle – a perfect present for a best friend!

A dazzling unicorn pendant

The secret of the unicorn's horn is found at its base – a beautiful red ruby. To give yourself the power of the unicorn, make this necklace that has a secret all of its own. You'll need:

* An old necklace chain or a piece of strong silvery thread
* A red-tinted sweet wrapper
* A small piece of card
* A red sweet, like a fruit pastille or wine gum
* Glue
* Foil
* A pair of scissors

1. First, make the setting for your necklace. Cut out an octagon — a shape with eight sides — from a piece of card that's a bit bigger than your sweet.

2. Cover this with foil, making sure that it's nice and smooth on the front.

3. Then ask an adult to make a hole near the top of the silver setting. This is to thread your chain through.

4. Wrap your special red sweet in the sweet wrapper. Then stick it on to the setting using a blob of glue.

5. Feed the chain through the hole and hang the pendant round your neck — a perfect pendant with a secret that's almost good enough to eat!